1008 GRAMS

1008 GRAMS

BRANDON BROOKS

PALMETTO
P U B L I S H I N G
Charleston, SC
www.PalmettoPublishing.com

Hardcover ISBN: 979-8-8229-4203-5
Paperback ISBN: 979-8-8229-4152-6

Contents

1008 Grams

Credit 4

Stock Market 9

Certificate Deposit 13

Small Businesses 16

Real Estate 21

Outro 24

    Rule #1: Strategic Defense 26

    Rule #2: Empower And Connect 26

    Rule #3: Embrace Wisdom. 27

    Rule #4: Remain Mysterious 27

Her. 31

    Physical 36

    Mental. 37

    Spiritual 39

    Summary 40

14 Laws of Growth: A Guide to Self-Development

Law I   Dream. 45

Law II   Invest 46

Law III   Study. 47

Law IV   Comprehend. 48

Law V   Grow. 50

Law VI   Reflect. 51

Contents

Law VII   Calculate.................................52

Law VIII Learn....................................53

Law IX   Observe..................................54

Law X   Read.....................................55

Law XI   Avoid....................................56

Law XI   Accountability...........................57

Law XIII Think....................................58

Law XIV Listen...................................59

Epilogue...63

Seven-Day Warrior

Introduction..67

Chapter I   Enemies..............................69

Chapter II   Goals................................71

Chapter III   Friends..............................73

Chapter IV   Weaknesses...........................75

Chapter V   Family...............................77

Chapter VI   Hobbies..............................79

Chapter VII Strengths............................80

Conclusion: Warrior.................................82

About the Author....................................83

Contact Information.................................84

WALNUT BOTTOM INVESTMENTS
PRESENTS

1008 GRAMS

In the realm of financial literature, "1008 Grams" stands as an enduring beacon, illuminating pathways to transformation and empowerment. Within its profound pages lies not merely a compendium of financial wisdom, but a sacred treasury of principles that transcend the mere accumulation of wealth. It serves as a guide, a mentor, and a philosopher, beckoning readers to embark on a journey of self-discovery, discipline, and mastery.

At its core, "1008 Grams" is a testament to the timeless virtues of prudence, diligence, and temperance. It is a call to arms against the relentless pursuit of material wealth at the expense of one's integrity and well-being. Through its teachings, readers are invited to transcend the fleeting temptations of consumerism and embrace a more profound understanding of prosperity—one rooted in financial acumen, ethical conduct, and holistic balance.

The essence of "1008 Grams" lies not in the mere acquisition of riches, but in the cultivation of a mindset—a mindset that views wealth not as an end in itself, but as a means to a greater purpose. It challenges readers to reevaluate their relationship with money, to see it not as a master to be served, but as a tool to be wielded with wisdom and discernment.

Beyond the confines of gender, "1008 Grams" explores the universal principles of dignity, grace, and reverence. It is a testament to the timeless art of mannerism and self-respect, reminding readers that true wealth lies not in the size of one's bank account, but in the depth of one's character. Through its pages, readers are called to embody these virtues, to walk with dignity, grace, and humility in all their dealings with others.

But "1008 Grams" is not merely a guide to financial success—it is a roadmap to spiritual enlightenment. It delves into the depths of the human soul, guiding readers toward alignment with higher callings and spiritual resonance. It is a beacon of light in a world shrouded in darkness, offering solace, guidance, and hope to all who seek it.

Through its timeless wisdom, "1008 Grams" empowers individuals to orchestrate a symphony of existence—a symphony that resounds with financial acumen, dignified conduct, spiritual harmony, and holistic equilibrium.

It is a legacy that transcends the bounds of time and space, leaving an indelible mark upon the chronicles of human history.

As you embark on your journey through the pages of "1008 Grams," may you find not only practical guidance for navigating the complexities of finance, but also profound insights into the nature of wealth, success, and fulfillment. May you emerge not only richer in material wealth, but also richer in wisdom, character, and purpose. And may the legacy you leave behind be one that resounds with dignity, grace, and reverence—a legacy worthy of the ages.

CREDIT

Establishing a strong credit profile is indeed a cornerstone of financial empowerment. Your credit score serves as a reflection of your financial responsibility and trustworthiness, influencing your ability to access various forms of credit and secure favorable terms on loans and other financial products.

To leverage your credit effectively, it's crucial to start by understanding the factors that contribute to your credit score. This includes making timely payments on your debts, maintaining a low credit utilization ratio, and managing a diverse mix of credit accounts responsibly.

By demonstrating a history of responsible borrowing and repayment, you can gradually build a positive credit history, which in turn can open doors to opportunities such as obtaining a mortgage, securing financing for a car or other major purchase, or even qualifying for lower insurance premiums.

However, it's important to remember that credit is a tool to be wielded with caution and prudence. While having access to credit can provide flexibility and convenience, it's essential to use it judiciously and avoid overextending yourself. Accumulating excessive debt or missing payments can have serious consequences for your credit score and financial well-being.

Ultimately, establishing a strong credit profile is about more than just numbers on a report—it's about cultivating responsible financial habits and building a foundation for long-term financial success. By prioritizing financial literacy, practicing disciplined money management, and leveraging credit wisely, you can set yourself on a path toward greater financial stability, security, and independence.

For individuals with savings but a less-than-ideal credit score, investing in improving their credit is not just a financial strategy—it's a pathway to greater financial freedom and opportunity.

Imagine you're someone who has diligently saved money over the years, perhaps through disciplined budgeting, automatic transfers to a savings account, or wise investment decisions. You've amassed a significant sum, providing you with a sense of security and peace of mind. However, despite your savings, your credit score tells a different story. Maybe you've had past financial setbacks, such as missed payments, high credit card balances, or even a bankruptcy, that have left a mark on your credit report.

In this scenario, having savings is undoubtedly a valuable asset, but without a strong credit profile, your options may be limited. A low credit score can hinder your ability to access credit when you need it most, whether it's for purchasing a home, buying a car, funding a business venture, or even covering unexpected expenses. Without access to credit, you may find yourself unable to take advantage of opportunities or navigate financial challenges effectively.

This is where investing in improving your credit becomes essential. By dedicating time, effort, and potentially some of your savings toward repairing and rebuilding your credit, you can unlock a world of possibilities. You can position yourself to qualify for better interest rates and terms on loans, saving you money in the long run. You can gain access to credit cards with rewards programs or perks that align with your lifestyle and financial goals. You can even improve your chances of securing rental housing or employment opportunities that require a credit check.

Investing in your credit is not just about boosting a number—it's about investing in yourself and your future. It's about demonstrating financial responsibility, resilience, and determination. It's about turning past setbacks into valuable lessons and opportunities for growth. And ultimately, it's about empowering yourself to achieve your dreams and aspirations, knowing that you have the financial foundation and freedom to pursue them.

So if you find yourself in a situation where you have savings but bad credit, don't despair. Instead, see it as an opportunity to invest in your financial well-being and set yourself on a path toward a brighter future. With dedication, patience, and perseverance, you can improve your credit score and unlock the doors to a world of possibilities.

A great credit score can be likened to a golden key that unlocks a multitude of financial benefits and opportunities. At its core, it signifies to lenders and creditors that you are a responsible borrower—a person who manages credit and debt obligations diligently and reliably. As a result, one of the primary advantages of having a great credit score is the access it grants you to credit products such as loans, credit cards, and lines of credit. Lenders are more inclined to extend credit to individuals with high credit scores, as they are perceived as lower-risk borrowers.

Moreover, a great credit score can translate into tangible savings through lower interest rates. When you apply for loans or credit cards, lenders use your credit score to assess the risk of lending to you. Borrowers with excellent credit scores are typically offered loans and credit cards with lower interest rates, meaning they pay less in interest over the life of the loan or when carrying a credit card balance. This can amount to significant savings over time, allowing you to keep more of your hard-earned money in your pocket.

In addition to favorable interest rates, a great credit score often results in higher credit limits. Lenders are more willing to extend larger lines of credit to individuals with strong credit histories, providing them with greater purchasing power and flexibility. Whether you're making a major purchase or covering unexpected expenses, having access to higher credit limits can offer peace of mind and financial security.

Beyond borrowing, a great credit score can positively impact other areas of your financial life. For example, landlords and property managers may conduct credit checks as part of the rental application process. A high credit score can increase your chances of being approved for rental housing, especially in competitive rental markets where landlords have numerous applicants to choose from. Similarly, some employers may review credit histories as part of the hiring process, particularly for positions that involve financial responsibilities or require security clearances. A great credit score can enhance your employability and credibility in the eyes of potential employers.

Furthermore, maintaining a great credit score can lead to lower insurance premiums. Many insurance companies use credit-based insurance scores to determine premiums for auto and homeowners insurance. Individuals with higher credit scores may qualify for lower insurance premiums, as they are perceived as lower-risk policyholders.

In addition to these benefits, having a great credit score can also stream-line everyday financial transactions. For example, utility companies may require customers with poor credit to pay a security deposit before acti-vating services such as electricity, water, or cable. However, individuals with excellent credit scores may be able to avoid these deposits altogether or have them waived.

Finally, a great credit score provides you with negotiating power when dealing with lenders, creditors, and service providers. Whether you're applying for a loan, negotiating a credit card interest rate, or discussing terms with a utility company, showcasing your stellar creditworthiness can put you in a stronger position to secure better terms, lower fees, or additional perks.

In summary, a great credit score is a valuable asset that offers a wide range of benefits and advantages. By maintaining responsible credit habits and managing your finances wisely, you can leverage your excellent credit score to access opportunities, save money, and enhance your overall financial well-being.

STOCK MARKET

The stock market stands as a dynamic arena where individuals converge to partake in the timeless ritual of exchanging ownership in businesses, symbolized by stocks or shares. These financial instruments, whether publicly traded on well-established exchanges or privately offered through emerging crowdfunding platforms, embody more than mere pieces of paper—they represent a tangible stake in the fortunes and endeavors of corporations, both large and small. Dividend stocks, in particular, hold a special allure for investors, promising a stream of regular payments derived from a company's profits—a passive income stream that speaks to the allure of financial independence and stability. However, the pursuit of dividend stocks is not without its challenges and complexities. It demands a careful and meticulous approach, requiring investors to scrutinize companies' financial health, track records of consistent payouts, and their ability to weather economic storms with resilience and fortitude.

For those venturing into the realm of investment with trepidation and uncertainty, Exchange-Traded Funds (ETFs) offer a compelling alternative. These diversified investment vehicles provide a convenient and accessible gateway to the world of investing, offering exposure to a broad array of assets, industries, and sectors within a single investment. With their simplicity, lower costs, and ease of understanding compared to traditional mutual funds, ETFs hold particular appeal for beginners seeking to build a diversified portfolio without the complexities of individual stock selection.

Yet, amidst the promise of dividend stocks and the simplicity of ETFs, the stoic mindset emerges as a guiding principle—a steadfast beacon amidst the tumultuous seas of market volatility and uncertainty. It reminds investors to approach the investment landscape with a disciplined perspective, grounded in rationality and resilience. Stoicism teaches us to acknowledge the inherent risks and uncertainties of investing, to accept the inevitability of market fluctuations, and to cultivate the mental fortitude necessary to weather the storms that may arise along the journey.

In summary, the stock market beckons as a realm of opportunity and potential, yet it also presents challenges and pitfalls that must be navigated with care and wisdom. Whether one's gaze falls upon the allure of dividend stocks or the simplicity of ETFs, embracing a stoic mindset is paramount. It is the cornerstone upon which informed decisions are made, risks are managed, and resilience is forged—a timeless philosophy that guides investors on the path towards financial independence and prosperity.

My approach to the stock market has been heavily influenced by studying the mindset of Charlie Munger and Warren Buffett. As I accumulated funds, I made it a habit to allocate money into my brokerage account and invest in stocks that piqued my interest. However, I quickly learned that successful investing requires more than just picking random stocks—I needed to commit to thorough research before making any investment decisions.

Like many beginners, I experienced losses when I first started trading. But instead of being discouraged, I viewed these losses as valuable learning experiences. They gave me the opportunity to gain hands-on experience and develop the confidence needed to navigate the complexities of the stock market. Each setback fueled my hunger to learn and improve, ultimately shaping me into a more resilient and knowledgeable investor.

Moving forward, I understand the importance of maintaining a disciplined approach to investing. I continue to prioritize thorough research and careful consideration before making any investment decisions. While my journey in the stock market has had its challenges, I'm committed to leveraging my experiences to make informed choices and pursue long-term success in the world of investing.

For beginners, I always advocate for starting with platforms they're familiar with, and Cash App is a prime example. Its user-friendly interface and accessibility make it an excellent entry point into the world of stock investing. In fact, I began my own trading journey while incarcerated in a federal prison, utilizing Cash App as my platform of choice.

As I grew more comfortable and confident in my abilities, I decided to expand my horizons. I withdrew my funds from Cash App and transitioned to a brokerage account with TD Ameritrade, now known as Charles Schwab. The transition allowed me access to a wider range of investment options and tools, empowering me to take my investing journey to the next level.

Before diving headfirst into the market, I always recommend beginners to take their time and familiarize themselves with the ups and downs of stock investing. Monitoring gains and losses, even on a simulated basis, can provide valuable insights into market dynamics and help build confidence in one's abilities.

Additionally, it's crucial to approach investing with a mindset of caution and prudence. I strongly advise against allocating any funds that you're not prepared to lose. The market can be unpredictable, and losses are an inevitable part of the journey. By starting small and gradually feeling your way into the market, you can mitigate risks and build a solid foundation for long-term success.

Partnering with a financial advisor can be a wise decision for gaining knowledge and expertise in navigating the complexities of the financial world. However, it's essential to remember that no one will care for your money as deeply as you will. This is why I always stress the importance of taking personal responsibility for your financial education and decisions.

Reading and learning about the market is invaluable, and I believe it's time well spent. One of the first books I delved into was "Stocks for Dummies." This comprehensive guide offers a breakdown of financial jargon, various trading styles, and strategies for accumulating wealth. By immersing yourself in literature that demystifies the market, you empower yourself with the knowledge and confidence needed to make informed decisions about your financial future.

Ultimately, while seeking advice from professionals is beneficial, nothing can replace the sense of empowerment that comes from understanding the market and taking control of your financial destiny. With dedication, education, and a commitment to continuous learning, you can navigate the complexities of the financial world with confidence and clarity.

Certificate Deposit

A certificate of deposit (CD) is a type of financial product offered by banks and credit unions. It operates similarly to a savings account, but with some key differences. When you open a CD, you agree to deposit a certain amount of money for a fixed period, known as the term or maturity period. This term can range from a few months to several years, depending on the terms offered by the financial institution.

During the term of the CD, the deposited funds are inaccessible without penalty. This means you cannot withdraw the money until the CD reaches its maturity date without facing a penalty fee, although some CDs offer early withdrawal options with associated penalties.

In exchange for locking up your funds for the agreed-upon term, banks typically offer higher interest rates on CDs compared to regular savings accounts. The interest rate is fixed for the duration of the CD term, providing certainty and predictability in the return on your investment.

The interest earned on a CD can be compounded at different intervals, such as daily, monthly, or annually, depending on the terms of the CD. At the end of the CD term, you receive both the initial deposit (principal) and the accumulated interest. This total amount is known as the CD's maturity value.

CDs offer a relatively low-risk investment option, as they are typically insured by the Federal Deposit Insurance Corporation (FDIC) or the National Credit Union Administration (NCUA) up to certain limits. This means that even if the issuing bank or credit union were to fail, your investment in the CD would be protected up to the insured limit.

In summary, a certificate of deposit (CD) is a financial product that allows you to earn a fixed interest rate on your deposit for a specified period, with the principal and interest returned to you at the end of the term. While CDs may offer higher interest rates compared to savings accounts, they require locking up funds for a predetermined period, making them best suited for individuals with a longer investment horizon and a desire for predictable returns.

When delving into the comparative analysis of returns garnered from traditional savings accounts versus those derived from certificate deposits (CDs), the divergence is palpable. Savings accounts often offer paltry returns, struggling to outpace the rate of inflation and thereby offering little in the way of meaningful growth potential. On the other hand, certificate deposits present a markedly different landscape, providing a more robust avenue for augmenting one's capital over a predetermined period.

The utilization of certificate deposits has emerged as a swift and efficient strategy for capitalizing on investment opportunities. The allure lies in the potential for more substantial returns, which, at present, hover around the 5% mark. This figure, however, is contingent upon the duration of the commitment. Shorter-term CDs may offer slightly lower returns, while longer-term CDs tend to yield higher rates. Consequently, investors are afforded the flexibility to tailor their investment horizon to suit their financial objectives and risk tolerance.

This method of investing represents a compelling option for those seeking a quick turnaround on their investments without the need for constant oversight or management. By locking in funds for a fixed period, investors can effectively hedge against market volatility while still capitalizing on higher interest rates. Furthermore, the hands-off nature of certificate deposits allows individuals to diversify their investment portfolio without the burden of continual monitoring or active decision-making.

In essence, understanding the intricacies of certificate deposits has unlocked a pathway to increasing wealth with minimal effort. By harnessing the power of this financial instrument, individuals can effectively capitalize on higher returns without the need for constant intervention. It represents a prudent and accessible means of growing one's capital, providing a reliable source of passive income and financial security in an ever-changing economic landscape.

I leverage certificate deposits as a strategic tool to amplify my savings swiftly. Here's how: I deposit my funds into a certificate deposit account for a predefined period, tapping into higher interest rates, typically averaging around 5%, contingent upon the length of my commitment. This approach enables me to effortlessly grow my savings while minimizing the need for constant oversight or management. It's a hands-off yet powerful method to maximize returns on my savings, providing me with a reliable and efficient way to boost my financial wealth.

Small Businesses

In the realm of entrepreneurship, small businesses serve as vessels for passion, innovation, and community impact—a pursuit steeped in stoic principles. They afford individuals the opportunity to carve their path, crafting something meaningful while contributing to the economic fabric of their community. Yet, beneath this veneer of promise lies a landscape fraught with challenges and uncertainties.

Launching a small business demands more than mere passion; it requires a resilient spirit and a strategic mindset. Financial uncertainty looms large, with the specter of market competition and operational hurdles casting a shadow over the journey. To navigate these treacherous waters, entrepreneurs must chart a course grounded in meticulous planning, astute financial management, and a profound understanding of their target audience.

But even the most well-laid plans can be derailed by regulatory complexities, staffing issues, or unforeseen market shifts. It is in these moments of adversity that the stoic ethos truly shines—a steadfast commitment to facing challenges with unwavering resolve and unwavering resolve. Successful small business owners are forged in the crucible of adversity, their mettle tested by the trials of entrepreneurship.

Yet, despite the myriad obstacles that lie in wait, the allure of small business ownership persists—a testament to the indomitable human spirit and the allure of forging one's destiny. For those bold enough to embark on this journey, the rewards are as bountiful as they are hard-earned. In the crucible of entrepreneurship, where passion meets resilience, lies the path to lasting success and fulfillment.

Profiting from your talents is a pathway to financial stability that I highly recommend. By embracing what you love to do and living in the moment, you can cultivate a lifestyle that truly fulfills you. In a world filled with distractions, it's essential to invest in yourself and pursue endeavors that positively impact your life.

One avenue to consider is publishing—actively making your knowledge, creativity, or expertise available to the public for sale or for free. Traditionally, this term referred to the creation and distribution of printed works like books, newspapers, and magazines. However, with the rise of digital information systems, the scope of publishing has expanded to include eBooks, digital magazines, websites, social media, music, and video game publishing.

Writing a book, for instance, presents a compelling opportunity to invest your time and expertise into creating a valuable asset that has the potential to generate passive income over time. A well-written and marketable book can yield royalties, licensing deals, and speaking engagements, contributing to your financial well-being in the long run. Furthermore, a successful book can enhance your reputation and unlock additional opportunities in your field.

However, it's important to recognize the risks involved. The success of a book as an investment is not guaranteed, and factors such as market demand, competition, and marketing strategies can significantly impact sales and overall returns. Additionally, the time and resources invested in the writing and publishing process may not yield immediate financial gains.

In summary, investing in writing a book requires a strategic approach that incorporates a thorough understanding of your target audience, effective marketing tactics, and a long-term perspective on potential returns. It's crucial to balance the creative process with a practical understanding of the publishing industry to maximize the financial benefits of your investment.

Another avenue to explore is selling photography online, which may not be the most obvious passive business opportunity but can offer scalability if done right. Platforms like Getty Images, Shutterstock, or Alamy allow you to license your photos for use, providing potential for recurring income each time someone downloads your images. By supplying high-demand photos, you can scale your efforts and potentially sell the same image hundreds or thousands of times, maximizing your earning potential.

Indeed, there are numerous avenues to generate wealth, and I wanted to highlight a few to provide readers with a glimpse of the possibilities available. By delving into options like writing a book or selling photography online, individuals can grasp a better understanding of the directions they may pursue to create financial stability and abundance.

It's disheartening to witness countless talented individuals underutilizing their skills and not providing services that the world could benefit from. There's a wealth of untapped potential waiting to be unleashed, and I urge readers to believe in themselves and their abilities.

Regardless of whether or not anyone purchases their content or products, it's crucial for individuals to continue building their catalog and leaving a legacy. By expressing themselves to the world through their creative endeavors, they not only enrich their own lives but also contribute to the collective tapestry of human experience.

So, to all the aspiring creators and entrepreneurs out there, believe in yourself. Trust in your talents and abilities. Don't let fear of failure hold you back. Keep creating, keep building, and keep sharing your gifts with the world. Your legacy awaits, and the impact you make will be felt far beyond your lifetime.

As you stand poised at the threshold of your entrepreneurial expedition, envision Gillian Brooks and her team at United and Equitable Solutions as your exclusive cadre of elite advisors. Gillian's dedication to mentorship and empowerment is not a mere sentiment—it's an invitation to join an esteemed circle of trailblazers. With an unparalleled understanding of the challenges and triumphs inherent in entrepreneurship, Gillian beckons aspiring visionaries to embark on a journey of exclusivity, navigating the intricate pathways of success with unwavering determination.

In her role as a global consultant, Gillian assumes a commanding position in sculpting the landscape of entrepreneurship on a global scale. Drawing upon her vast reservoir of expertise and insights, she curates bespoke strategies that empower businesses to transcend boundaries and achieve unparalleled success. From meticulously analyzing market dynamics to crafting personalized growth plans, Gillian's guidance serves as a beacon of exclusivity in an ever-expanding marketplace.

But Gillian's influence extends far beyond conventional business realms. At her core lies a commitment to nurturing a culture of innovation and excellence. As a mentor and advocate for entrepreneurship, she invites aspiring leaders into an exclusive enclave of visionaries, instilling in them a sense of confidence and resilience that sets them apart from the crowd.

In essence, Gillian Brooks emerges as a guardian of exclusivity, a purveyor of growth, innovation, and empowerment in the realm of entrepreneurship. Her dedication to uplifting others and her unwavering commitment to excellence make her an indispensable ally to United and Equitable Solutions and the global community of aspiring leaders.

So, if you find yourself yearning for exclusivity in your entrepreneurial journey, heed the call of Gillian Brooks and her team. With their unparalleled expertise and exclusive guidance, success becomes not just a distant dream, but an exclusive privilege reserved for the select few. Together, let us embark on an exclusive journey of growth and achievement, leaving an indelible mark on the world of entrepreneurship.

REAL ESTATE

Real estate investments present unparalleled opportunities for wealth accumulation and financial stability. Whether in residential, commercial, or industrial properties, real estate offers avenues for capital appreciation, steady rental income, and favorable tax treatment. Unlike other asset classes, real estate investments provide tangible assets with inherent value, offering investors a sense of security and stability.

One of the key advantages of real estate investment is its potential for long-term appreciation. Historically, real estate values have tended to increase over time, providing investors with a hedge against inflation and a source of wealth accumulation. Additionally, rental properties offer a reliable income stream, providing investors with passive cash flow to supplement their earnings and build wealth over time.

Moreover, real estate investments offer tax advantages that can enhance overall returns. Deductions for mortgage interest, property taxes, depreciation, and other expenses can significantly reduce taxable income, allowing investors to keep more of their rental income and maximize their profits.

Despite the potential benefits, real estate investment requires careful consideration and strategic planning. Investors must conduct thorough due diligence, analyze market trends, and assess potential risks before making investment decisions. Additionally, effective property management practices are essential to maximize returns and mitigate risks associated with vacancy, maintenance, and tenant turnover.

In conclusion, real estate investment offers a compelling opportunity for investors to build wealth, diversify their portfolios, and achieve long-term financial success. With proper research, prudent decision-making, and diligent management, investors can capitalize on the inherent advantages of real estate to achieve their investment objectives and secure their financial futures.

After thorough discussions with my CPA and diligent preparation in building a robust credit rating and stable income stream, I am now poised to embark on real estate investment ventures. My steadfast commitment to rental properties stems from extensive research conducted during my time in federal prison two years ago. I am resolute in my desire for my home to serve as an asset rather than a liability, avoiding the long-term commitment of a traditional 30-year mortgage. Instead, I aspire to leverage real estate to facilitate my passion for global exploration, immersing myself in diverse cultures and gaining insights into alternative wealth-building strategies.

My unwavering determination is fueled by a deep-seated desire to provide opportunities to others that I myself may not have had access to. I am steadfast in my resolve to contribute positively to the world by creating pathways for financial empowerment and prosperity. Through prudent real estate investments and a commitment to embracing cultural diversity, I aim to foster greater understanding, connectivity, and abundance for myself and those around me.

Entering the realm of real estate investment is indeed a promising opportunity, one that offers the potential for substantial financial rewards and personal fulfillment. Your readiness to tackle any obstacles that may arise along the way is a testament to your resilience and determination, key qualities that will serve you well in this venture.

As you venture into real estate investment, it's commendable that you're also exploring opportunities in land acquisition. Land investments offer unique advantages, including the potential for future development and appreciation. By diversifying your investment portfolio to include both real estate and land assets, you position yourself for greater flexibility and growth potential.

While the journey ahead may present challenges, your proactive mindset and willingness to learn and adapt will be invaluable assets. By staying informed, seeking guidance from experienced professionals, and remaining focused on your long-term goals, you'll be well-equipped to navigate the complexities of the real estate market and capitalize on the opportunities it presents.

Embrace this new chapter with confidence and determination, knowing that each obstacle you overcome brings you one step closer to achieving your vision of financial success and security. With perseverance and a strategic approach, the world of real estate and land investment holds boundless potential for growth and prosperity.

Outro

In the vast expanse of financial opportunities, many stand at the crossroads, uncertain of which path to tread. To those seeking direction, I offer guidance rooted in knowledge and encouragement to embark on the journey toward financial independence.

Education serves as the cornerstone of confidence in navigating the complexities of personal finance and investment. Through diligent research and continuous learning, individuals arm themselves with the tools needed to make informed decisions and seize opportunities with conviction.

Yet, the journey toward financial freedom is not without its trials. Challenges will arise, doubts will cloud the path, and obstacles will seem insurmountable. In these moments, resilience becomes our greatest ally, propelling us forward and reminding us that giving up is never an option.

Preservation of resolve in the face of adversity is paramount. It demands inner strength, unwavering determination, and a steadfast commitment to our goals. By embracing challenges as opportunities for growth, we harness the power of perseverance to propel us toward our aspirations.

In the pursuit of financial success and personal growth, cultivating a resilient mindset is essential. The principles outlined in resources like the 14 Laws of Growth offer invaluable insights into shaping the mental framework needed for achievement. Through dedication and self-awareness, we nurture a mindset characterized by determination and resilience.

Maintaining focus amidst distractions is crucial for progress. By limiting external influences and staying committed to our goals, we channel our energy toward meaningful endeavors aligned with our vision.

Accountability serves as a guiding principle on our journey, urging us to take ownership of our actions and decisions. Through self-accountability, we foster responsibility and empower ourselves to pursue our goals with purpose and determination.

Ultimately, achieving financial success requires discipline, dedication, and a steadfast commitment to self-improvement. Embracing challenges with resilience and continuously striving for excellence, we unlock our full potential and forge a path toward the life we envision.

RULE #1: STRATEGIC DEFENSE

In any conflict or endeavor, the foundation of success lies in a meticulously crafted defense. This defense encompasses a multifaceted approach, integrating technological prowess, strategic deployment, and logistical preparedness. Each element is crucial, from the sophistication of military resources to the provision of sustenance for resilience. Shelter, too, must be fortified strategically to protect personnel and assets. Furthermore, harnessing natural resources not only provides a tactical advantage but also fosters self-reliance and sustainability. Thus, a comprehensive defense strategy, marked by the astute utilization of resources, is indispensable for navigating challenges with professionalism and resilience.

RULE #2: EMPOWER AND CONNECT

The establishment of personal influence hinges on empowering others and fostering meaningful connections. Actively creating opportunities that positively impact lives solidifies your role as a catalyst for positive change. Strategic alliances amplify collective strength, extending networks beyond individual capabilities. Pursuing knowledge and understanding human behavior are pivotal in becoming irreplaceable. Enriching skills and comprehending interpersonal dynamics propel a trajectory of influence and impact.

RULE #3: EMBRACE WISDOM

Life's journey demands a holistic exploration, encompassing the discovery of purpose, the embrace of spirituality, and the astute management of resources. Beyond financial assets, wealth encompasses a mindful alignment of resources with life's purpose. Delving into purpose, spirituality, and resourcefulness fosters a life rich in meaningful experiences and purposeful connections.

RULE #4: REMAIN MYSTERIOUS

In the intricate theater of strategic endeavors, the enigmatic allure of a man who adeptly cloaks himself in mystery emerges as a formidable asset. This deliberate cultivation of an aura of unpredictability extends its influence across various facets, from tactical decision-making to the overarching intentions guiding his maneuvers.

The deliberate withholding of crucial information and the nuanced art of unpredictability act as potent psychological tools, injecting an air of unease into the minds of adversaries. This calculated approach not only keeps rivals off balance but also disrupts their capacity to formulate coherent responses. It is within the deliberate dance of revealing only the essential and concealing the intricate layers of strategy that a man of mystery crafts a compelling presence, navigating the complexities of strategic engagements with finesse and gaining a distinct advantage in the intricate chessboard of calculated maneuvers.

"Embrace humility in the presence of those who possess greater knowledge and expertise in specific areas. Their insights and experiences are invaluable assets that can enrich your own understanding. Approach interactions with a willingness to learn, asking thoughtful questions that yield meaningful answers. Remember, true wisdom comes from a humble and receptive attitude towards acquiring knowledge."

"Take ownership of your decisions and actions, and hold yourself accountable for your choices. Rather than making excuses, focus on finding solutions to overcome challenges. By addressing issues head-on and redirecting your energy towards meaningful endeavors, you can stay committed to your goals and responsibilities, paving the way for success and fulfillment."

"Surround yourself with those who uplift and support your journey. Shed the weight of negativity and envy, for it only serves to hold you back. Recognize your own worth and refuse to settle for anything less than what you deserve. Embrace the company of those who inspire you to reach greater heights, and watch as you prosper with unwavering determination and clarity of purpose."

"Knowledge is the ultimate tool for success. Through the simple act of reading, we unlock endless possibilities for growth and self-improvement. By immersing ourselves in books on various subjects, we expand our understanding of the world and deepen our insight into human behavior. With each page turned, we sharpen our intellect and empower ourselves to navigate life's challenges with clarity and confidence. Embrace the journey of lifelong learning, for it is the key to unlocking your fullest potential."

"Observation is the key to understanding. By keenly observing the behaviors and habits of those around us, we gain invaluable insights into their character and motivations. Armed with this knowledge, we can navigate social interactions with wisdom and foresight, staying three steps ahead in every situation."

"Comparison is the thief of joy. Embrace your uniqueness and individual journey, for therein lies your true purpose. By pursuing your passions with unwavering dedication, you illuminate the path to self-discovery and fulfillment."

"Adaptation is the cornerstone of resilience. In the face of uncertainty, we must learn to navigate with precision and clarity, making decisions grounded in reason rather than emotion. Embrace calculated designs and rational thinking, for they pave the way to wisdom and enlightenment."

"Reflection is the compass that guides us on the path of self-discovery and growth. By pausing to ponder our actions and choices, we gain clarity and insight into what truly matters. Embrace the power of reflection, for it is the key to unlocking your full potential."

"Letting go of resentment is not about excusing someone's behavior; it's about freeing yourself from the burden of carrying their actions with you. Forgiveness is a gift you give yourself, allowing you to move forward with strength and grace."

"Setting boundaries is not an act of selfishness; it's an act of self-respect. By defining your limits, you protect your mental, emotional, and physical well-being, allowing yourself to flourish in healthy relationships."

"True fulfillment in any relationship stems from a foundation built on love, trust, honesty, and mutual respect. Beyond materialistic ideals, it's essential to recognize and honor a woman's worth by understanding her aspirations, strengths, and vulnerabilities. Communication and empathy are key to fostering meaningful connections and nurturing genuine love. Let us transcend societal illusions and embrace the profound beauty of authentic human connection."

"Knowledge is the currency of wealth. By investing in learning and mastering the art of financial allocation, we unlock the door to prosperity. Study, research, and invest wisely—let your money work for you and pave the path to abundance."

"Amidst life's distractions, discipline becomes our compass, guiding us back to our goals, dreams, and aspirations. Surround yourself with those who uplift and support your journey, for together, we rise."

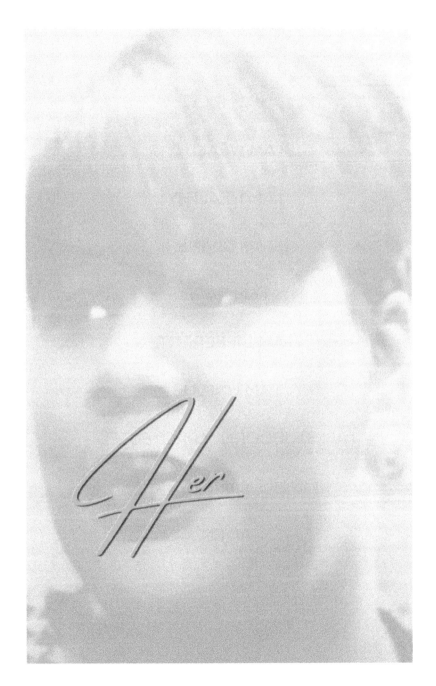

31

I AM RICH.

I AM WEALTHY.

I AM HEALTHY.

I AM DIVINE.

I AM RARE.

I AM DIFFERENT.

I AM UNIQUE.

I AM STUBBORNLY PROTECTED.

IN HIS NAME I PRAY!

AMEN.

As a woman, it is imperative for you to create dominance in your presence. Your behaviors have to be aligned with your thoughts, and your beliefs should stand on loyalty, respect, integrity, and honor. Practice self-worth by setting boundaries with both men and women. Let the aura that surrounds you demand respect. Display mannerisms that reflect humility and modesty. Avoid promiscuous behaviors and avoid false perceptions by analyzing scenarios with others prior to engagement. Strive to participate in acts of service within your community. Doing so will help you find balance and peace within yourself.

As you strive to find your purpose, you will begin to feel complete. You will walk with confidence and determination as those around you will show you the highest level of respect and admiration. You will feel serene and refreshed in providing the best version of self. Moving towards prioritizing your direction in life, you will reap the benefits from the discipline you've had instilled in yourself throughout your life course.

As humans, we must develop self-control regarding our actions and behaviors. Take the initiative to distance yourself from others who are highly captivated by social influence. Avoid being entertained by "what's acceptable" to society as a whole and create your own journey, your own path, with the core values of reflection, application, and perseverance. Lock in on your goals and surround yourself with productive engagements that will contribute to your personal growth.

It is important to set attainable goals to reach your full potential. While gaining the approval of your peers is not a necessity, setting and surpassing the limits you've set for yourself will impact your character in a positive way. Those around you will notice the progression taking place in your life and you will earn their respect and admiration.

Understanding the structure behind setting goals is important. Positioning yourself to surpass the boundaries that once blocked your advancement will catapult you to new heights. Each victory will cause you to seek higher elevations in your pursuits. Your sheer determination and courage to face any obstacle will cause you to push through whatever threatens to block your blessings. The outcome will be obvious to those around you, and you will continue to produce motion. You will be able to reflect on the fact that you've reached your goal, and setting new goals will assist you in expanding and developing additional values that will give you deeper insight into your true identity. You set the standard for YOU! Do not give that power to anyone else, for it does not belong to others to make you who they want you to be.

"A prominent woman with grace and eloquence"

Grasping the concept of understanding the power of presentation is remarkable. Learning different ways to influence the thoughts of others can be useful when dealing with scenarios you may be unfamiliar with. Observe those around you. Remember to take note of your opponent's weaknesses when entering a room. Understand that in most cases you will be perceived one way, but remain true to yourself. Remain classy, yet professional. Redirect any energy that you don't appreciate in a stoic manner. Be assertive and adamant about your opinions, and never undermine your intuition.

Examine others carefully. Let their behaviors show you who they are. Dissect what they say while analyzing their attitudes. Refuse to create a family with a man who is not goal-oriented or who is incapable of leading. He will become a burden on your journey to happiness. Instead of experiencing joy, you will be fixated on trying to endure the agony of betrayal. Trying to love others before you love yourself is not possible. Until you find a man who is worthy of being in your presence, you do not need to be submissive or loyal.

"He who honors his wife will live a righteous life."

Being absorbed by a force generated remotely by the One above, I was positioned to experience a relationship that allowed me to respect the worth of a woman. I watched her navigate her way around any room she occupied, I also calculated her every move, I was captivated by her very existence. The consistency and resilience of this living being caused me to observe the mysterious air that surrounded her. I began to reflect on the chemistry we could create in the days that followed. Suddenly, I became intrigued by her intellect and her mannerisms as she worked the room.

PHYSICAL

Physical exercise, diet, and self-care practices are essential to our well-being. By committing to these practices, we can create a better understanding of the causes and effects of our overall health.

Humans should remain diligent when it comes to establishing healthier patterns. Engaging in exercise releases dopamine, a neurotransmitter associated with pleasure, motivation, and hope. Aerobic exercise and cardio training are particularly effective in boosting these feelings.

To reduce stress and maintain mental clarity, it is crucial to follow a consistent schedule that includes ample rest. Waking up at the same time every day reinforces the body's sleep-wake cycle, enhancing overall performance.

A balanced diet is vital for absorbing essential vitamins, minerals, and nutrients to support both physical and mental health. Adequate hydration is also crucial for transporting nutrients and improving digestion, which helps fight off diseases.

Formulating an action plan for maintaining health is imperative. Implementing a proper self-care routine activates the parasympathetic nervous system, leading to the release of serotonin and dopamine. Serotonin, another neurotransmitter, regulates bodily functions and contributes to overall well-being.

MENTAL

Self-acceptance, loyalty, resilience, and leadership are characteristics of the brave. It is my belief that as we take the time to analyze a person who embodies these elements, we subconsciously not only gravitate to them but ultimately, are influenced by their efforts to persevere through adversity with poise and confidence.

Learning to accept ourselves comes from understanding ourselves fully. This means comprehending our strengths, weaknesses, and capabilities. As we grow, we must adapt to situations, circumstances, and opportunities, being aware, alert, and prepared to execute our goals accordingly. If one does not understand oneself, how can one fulfill obligations? That's why it's crucial to dissect and discover our core beliefs to understand why we think and behave the way we do.

Our beliefs primarily stem from our thoughts, which dictate our actions. Understanding what loyalty entails is vital to our growth. Acknowledging loyalty helps us grasp our morals, principles, core values, and beliefs. Embracing experiences provides different outlooks on life and helps us navigate acts of betrayal from others. We must evaluate what loyalty means to us, analyze who deserves our loyalty, and avoid betrayal from those who pose as friends but act as enemies.

Learning to withstand or recover quickly from adversity is key. When we adopt this mindset, we become assets to ourselves and others. We must utilize our challenges to penetrate and destroy obstacles in our way, learning from each situation and implementing strategies to avoid similar issues in the future.

Developing leadership skills involves strategic yet assertive behavior, thorough analysis of others' behaviors, anticipation of different outcomes, and creation of beneficial opportunities. Great leaders are created through training and preparation, not born from the womb. As we grow, we must be mindful of how our actions affect others and surround ourselves with rational thinkers who manage emotions effectively. Effective communication is crucial, as it transforms us from liabilities to assets in any situation.

SPIRITUAL

In theory, spiritual practices related to self-reflection include reading, praying, journaling, and meditating. These actions allow you to embrace spiritual growth and gain structure and alertness. Reading offers an opportunity to absorb knowledge and reflect on daily beliefs, strategies, and religion, leading to a sense of fulfillment.

Prayer enables prosperity through the relationship established with oneself. Understanding my passion, I express myself through journaling thoughts, fostering internal growth, and coping with past problems. This coping mechanism positions me for success and growth.

There may come a time when you feel misunderstood on Earth, creating an impenetrable circle surrounded by goals, beliefs, and ideas. With a sense of direction and purpose, you live with urgency.

"We love and grow to obtain and persevere; in the midst of victory, we declare war."

Meditation aligns us spiritually with our inner selves, fostering relaxation, focus, clarity, and guidance. With precision, we aim for truth.

Summary

"There are times when humans feel incomplete due to misunderstanding. Knowing your self-worth allows you to comprehend that you are complete, even outside a relationship with a significant other. Recognizing self-worth creates immeasurable confidence.

Be someone who is respectful, honest, modest, authentic, intelligent, loyal, pure, assertive, caring, and brave. After reading this book, you should understand that implementing boundaries as a woman means honoring yourself as an individual with an understanding of your needs and wants.

Without boundaries, we allow others to override our feelings and desires. Reinforce boundaries in an assertive manner with a serious tone, proper eye contact, and chaste gestures.

Individuals lacking boundaries often struggle to express true feelings about a person, situation, or circumstance. A good starting point for a woman is writing down qualities and behaviors that make her happiest, acknowledging these qualities as non-negotiable. When establishing boundaries, resistance, often in the form of anger, may arise. People with boundary issues have character defects. When dealing with those who don't respect boundaries, accept that you can't control them and immediately detach yourself.

NEVER COMPROMISE LOVING YOURSELF.

Acknowledging the law of attraction, I recognize that when I started entertaining a healthier lifestyle, I began to value life more."

"I attracted people who had similar values, goals, challenges, and intentions, allowing me to protect my peace. I began to realize unfamiliar opportunities but also encountered resistance. Then, I took the time to elevate, reflect, and be grateful. Now, the opportunities aren't so unfamiliar.

What was uncomfortable was leaving people behind—those who were a distraction, those filled with envy, those incapable of loving me, and those unable to understand my new journey. As humans, we can get so caught up in others' thoughts that we neglect blessings from above.

For the first time, I live in harmony with my thoughts, actions, feelings, and beliefs."

Walnut Bottom Investments LLC. is company engaged in the business of dealing with financial and monetary transactions such as deposits, loans, investments and, currency exchange. Walnut Bottom Investments LLC. encompass a broad range of business operations within the financial services sector including banks, trust companies, insurance companies, brokerage firms, and investment dealers. Walnut Bottom Investments LLC. offers a wide range of products and services for individual and commercial clients. Walnut Bottom Investments LLC. is here to help you get an optimal investment solution that aligns with your goals. Investment goals are personal, but no matter what are you trying to achieve, it is critical to take an objective look ahead. Accomplish your goals, and formulate your financial objectives.

14

LAWS

OF

GROWTH

A GUIDE TO SELF-DEVELOPMENT

BRANDON BROOKS

LAW I

Dream

As humans, we encounter distractions on a daily basis, tempting us to veer off course from our goals, dreams, and ideas. Therefore, it is essential that we cultivate discipline within ourselves to stay focused amidst these distractions. Additionally, surrounding ourselves with supportive individuals who encourage our growth and development is crucial. By maintaining this discipline and fostering a supportive environment, we fortify our resolve and remain steadfast on the path towards achieving our aspirations.

LAW II

Invest

To amass wealth, acquiring knowledge on investing is paramount. While many are conditioned to save diligently, the true path to wealth lies in learning how to allocate your resources strategically. By understanding how to invest wisely, you empower your money to generate additional income for you. This shift from mere savings to strategic investment is the cornerstone of building lasting wealth and financial independence.

Study, research, and invest!

LAW III

Study

The cornerstone of personal growth lies in the study of oneself. This entails identifying one's strengths and weaknesses while cultivating morals and principles grounded in integrity. By embarking on this introspective journey, individuals gain profound insight into their character, motivations, and values. Through continuous self-examination, they can refine their behaviors, enhance their virtues, and navigate life with clarity and purpose. Ultimately, the pursuit of self-understanding serves as the foundation for leading a fulfilling and virtuous existence.

Analyze, learn, and transform!

LAW IV

Comprehend

In any relationship, whether with a man or a woman, certain key elements are essential: love, trust, honesty, consistency, and honor. Additionally, individuals should embody characteristics of ambition, eloquence, and modesty. It is crucial for both men and women to recognize and appreciate a woman's inherent worth beyond superficial attributes or material possessions.

Too often, societal influences distort our perception of a woman's identity, leading to the propagation of false ideals. It is imperative to challenge these illusions and instead invest time in understanding a woman's aspirations, strengths, weaknesses, preferences, dreams, and past experiences. This includes delving into her personal definitions of love, commitment, respect, and loyalty.

Reflecting on my upbringing in Baltimore, Maryland, I acknowledge that I was not taught to approach relationships with women in this manner. Regrettably, I subjected them to emotional, physical, and verbal abuse due to my own lack of self-love and understanding. I failed to grasp the significance of effective communication, boundaries, and the true essence of friendship. It is only through introspection and growth that I have come to recognize the importance of treating women with the care, respect, and understanding they deserve.

LAW V

Grow

Focusing on circumstances, predicaments, and individuals beyond our control is fruitless. Similarly, holding onto resentment towards those who have caused us pain serves no purpose. Instead, channel your energy towards endeavors within your sphere of influence and cultivate inner peace by letting go of grudges. In doing so, you free yourself from unnecessary burdens and empower yourself to focus on what truly matters for your growth and well-being.

Forgive, persevere, and grow!

LAW VI

Reflect

It is essential to cultivate the habit of reflecting on our daily behaviors, conversations, and decisions. By integrating the "reflection factor" into our lives, we shield ourselves from engaging in situations that do not align with our path to success. Through introspection and thoughtful analysis, we discern which actions serve our goals and which detract from them. Embracing this practice empowers us to navigate life with clarity and purpose, ensuring that every step we take propels us closer to our desired outcomes.

LAW VII

Calculate

As we embark on the journey of reestablishment, it becomes imperative to navigate with agility and adaptability. We must craft meticulous strategies with swiftness and precision, all while adhering to rational thinking and eschewing decisions driven by emotions. Mastering this skill enables us to minimize errors and attain genuine comprehension of the reasoning behind our choices. Through deliberate and methodical actions, we pave the way for a path of clarity and purpose.

LAW VIII

Learn

When we dedicate ourselves to understanding life's intricacies, we gain clarity on our own essence. As humans, we often find ourselves comparing our journeys to those of others. However, each of us harbors unique aspirations and views on success and fulfillment. By directing our focus towards our passions, we unlock the path to discovering our true purpose in life. It is through this pursuit of what ignites our soul that we align ourselves with our most authentic selves and forge our own distinct path to fulfillment.

Self-love, self-respect, and self-worth!

LAW IX

Observe

One of the most profound lessons I learned was from an individual in Louisiana, originally from Baltimore, Maryland. He possessed an unparalleled level of observation, consistently emphasizing throughout our discussions that people reveal their true selves through their actions.

Since that enlightening encounter, I've embraced the practice of keenly observing individuals with precision. By paying attention to various aspects of their lives—such as their associations, conversations, attire, purchases, leisure activities, and reading material—I've gained invaluable insights into their character.

By steadfastly adhering to this approach to life, one can greatly benefit. I wholeheartedly endorse the adoption of this principle. Always strive to stay three steps ahead, equipped with the foresight to navigate interactions with those around you effectively.

LAW X

Read

One of the most prevalent errors people make in life is neglecting to cultivate a habit of continuous learning through reading. To achieve financial stability, delve into books on financial literacy. For personal growth, immerse yourself in self-help literature. Sharpen your mind and perpetuate mental growth without bounds. The pursuit of knowledge knows no limits. Stay informed about world events and the intricacies of human behavior. By consistently seeking understanding and broadening your perspective, you empower yourself to navigate life's complexities with wisdom and insight.

The more you know, the easier life will be!

LAW XI

Avoid

Detach yourself from the inauthentic and the envious. Surround yourself only with those who genuinely support and celebrate your achievements. There is no benefit in associating with individuals who do not wish you well; they only serve to impede your progress. Despite recognizing the signs of their negativity in their actions, we often cling to these individuals. Embrace the wisdom to discern between genuine allies and those who hinder your growth. By choosing to align yourself solely with those who uplift and empower you, you pave the way for your own success and fulfillment.

Understand your worth.
Detach immediately.
Prosper hastily.

LAW XII

Accountability

Accepting responsibility for our actions is paramount. Observing the actions of those around us provides valuable insights into our own behavior. Excuses serve only to divert attention from the task at hand; instead, focus on solving the problem directly. By addressing challenges with proactive solutions, we conserve valuable energy that can be channeled into fulfilling our commitments and obligations. In the face of adversity, embrace a resolute mindset, unwavering in the pursuit of solutions and progress.

Accept, solve, and progress!

LAW XIII

Think

Indeed, obtaining information may seem straightforward, yet acquiring truly useful knowledge is a more formidable task. It requires the implementation of humility, especially in the presence of individuals who possess greater expertise in specific areas. Recognize the invaluable insights they can offer, stemming from their experiences and wisdom. Master the art of asking questions that yield the answers you seek, thereby maximizing the benefits of their knowledge. In embracing humility and respecting the expertise of others, one gains access to priceless wisdom that can profoundly shape one's path to growth and understanding.

Manipulative yet strategic!

LAW XIV

Listen

In the summer of 2018, at the age of twenty-eight, I crossed paths with a man from Philadelphia, Pennsylvania. Driven by a relentless pursuit of personal advancement, I sought knowledge that would distinguish me from the crowd. Engaging in conversations with this individual revealed a crucial truth: true elevation necessitates a willingness to listen and accept constructive criticism. Embracing this advice propelled me to progress in ways I had never envisioned.

This newfound approach enabled me to glean valuable insights from various individuals throughout my journey. Their wisdom not only transformed my outlook on life but also significantly influenced my approach to business.

During my time incarcerated, I formed a profound friendship with a man from Brooklyn, New York. His unwavering encouragement motivated me to strive for excellence, fostering a deep sense of camaraderie between us. Though his guidance was often subtle, it provided me with invaluable perspectives on manhood and personal conduct. As a rational thinker, he recognized my potential and wholeheartedly invested in my growth.

One day, I encountered a man from Greenville, North Carolina, a mathematical genius and business guru. He stood as the most intellectually engaging individual I've had the privilege to build a personal connection with. His understanding of growth and genuine concern for others made him an invaluable presence in my life. Through his actions, he exemplified the importance of giving one's all and persevering through adversity, demonstrating that growth knows no bounds.

Another man, hailing from Charlotte, North Carolina, became akin to a brother to me. His unwavering loyalty and actions spoke volumes about true love and support. His presence prompted me to reevaluate the relationships in my life, urging me to prioritize self-love and personal development on the path to success.

Unexpectedly, I found common ground with a man from Philadelphia, Pennsylvania, through the game of chess. Despite his origins, he exuded humility in every interaction, treating everyone with respect and dignity. His demeanor inspired me to cultivate a similar sense of humility, fostering deeper spiritual connections with others. These encounters have profoundly shaped my journey, instilling valuable lessons of perseverance, self-reflection, and humility.

One of the greatest leaders I ever met showed me the power of influence. He was a shrewd businessman, and one of the most influential figures I have ever met in my life. He taught me the laws of leadership, and I appreciate the conversations we had. I observed his behaviors daily, which gave me greater insight on the power of leadership. These experiences were truly a blessing and help me gain a better understanding of things I needed to work on.

The most highly respected man I ever met was from Puerto Rico. He helped me understand the value of structure. He allocated responsibility accordingly, and he took advantage of every opportunity that came his way. He was savvy and consciously understanding of the people around him. He was quick to position people to their strengths and gave them many opportunities to succeed. As I grew learning how to listen, I invited opportunities to come my way.

One of the greatest leaders I ever met, originating from Puerto Rico, exemplified the formidable power of influence despite serving a lengthy federal sentence followed by a state bid. He was a shrewd businessman, undeniably one of the most influential figures I've encountered. Through our conversations, he imparted invaluable lessons on the laws of leadership, for which I am deeply grateful. Observing his behaviors daily provided profound insights into the dynamics of leadership. These experiences were indeed a blessing, offering clarity on areas requiring refinement and personal growth.

He instilled in me the importance of structure, skillfully allocating responsibilities and seizing every opportunity that crossed his path. With an astute awareness of those around him, he adeptly positioned individuals according to their strengths, providing ample opportunities for success. As I refined my ability to listen and learn, I actively cultivated opportunities, following his strategic guidance.

Epilogue

After reading this book, it's important to recognize its purpose: to provide daily motivation, courage, and wisdom for those committed to growth. I strongly encourage you to devote five to ten minutes each day revisiting the laws and quotes contained within. By integrating these principles into your daily routine, you'll gain a deeper understanding of their significance and relevance to your life. Embrace a commitment to self-awareness, striving to comprehend both yourself and those around you more fully. Through consistent practice and reflection, you'll cultivate the resilience and insight necessary to navigate life's challenges with purpose and clarity.

Transform, live, and excel!

Enjoy and thank you for your support!
#FreeTheRealJoeBoy

Seven-Day Warrior

BY BRANDON BROOKS

Introduction

Victory at all costs, victory in spite of all terror,
victory however long and hard the road may be;
for without victory, there is no survival.
—Winston Churchill

Our aim? Victory. This book endeavors to instill discipline and structure within oneself. As we commit to this way of living, we embark on a journey of restarting, refocusing, and redirecting toward a better life. Embracing change may seem daunting, but by adopting this mindset, we initiate clarity, meaning, and purpose in our pursuit of success.

CHAPTER I

Enemies

*A team doesn't win the championship if its players
are working from different agendas.*
—John C. Maxwell

Understanding the identity of our adversaries holds paramount importance. They camouflage themselves, masquerading as friends, family, and partners. When we fail to discern their true nature, they insidiously infiltrate our lives. It is imperative to scrutinize both the words and actions of those around us, observing their behavior meticulously. Envy, often subconscious, emanates from individuals in our midst daily. Yet, we frequently overlook the signs they exhibit, rendering ourselves vulnerable to betrayal. We may grant them the benefit of the doubt, despite glimpses of their true selves. Through careful observation and analysis, we unravel their facade, discerning their authentic essence. Upon reaching this juncture, it becomes imperative to swiftly sever ties with these individuals, safeguarding our progress and well-being.

When we welcome individuals who lack our best interests into our lives, we invite stagnation to infiltrate our path. This compromises our ability to seize progressive moments on our journey toward greatness. Therefore, it is imperative to be discerning in our associations, ensuring that those we surround ourselves with uplift and support our endeavors. By maintaining a circle of allies who genuinely have our best interests at heart, we create an environment conducive to growth and achievement.

CHAPTER II

Goals

As people we need goals so that we can galvanize them.
—John C. Maxwell

Your goals serve as the compass guiding your journey. Success stems directly from the goals you set for yourself. As we evolve, we cultivate self-discipline to not only commit to these goals but also to achieve them. However, amidst the myriad distractions of modern life, we often find ourselves prioritizing situations and circumstances that do not contribute to our growth and development.

Embracing these distractions breeds complacency, hindering our progress. Adopting the mindset of a warrior necessitates focus and relinquishing unproductive habits. Instead, we embrace a healthier lifestyle conducive to monitoring our progress effectively. Understanding the underlying reasons behind our goals is crucial, as it allows us to grasp the significance of our endeavors.

When we embark on our journey, we inevitably encounter individuals who share similar desires and ambitions. These like-minded individuals serve as companions on our path to success, reinforcing our determination and providing support along the way.

The solution lies in rising early and heading to the library to study. As you establish this routine, you'll encounter others dedicated to the same goal. The consistency, ambition, and commitment to this routine are paramount. Embrace those around you who share your drive and build with them. Understand their challenges, goals, and dreams, fostering a support system where each member holds the other accountable. As we evolve, it becomes imperative to distance ourselves from anyone or anything hindering our growth. As we conclude, ask yourself: What do you aim to achieve in life?

CHAPTER III

Friends

Character makes trust possible.
—John C. Maxwell

It is my belief that expectations are often overlooked in friendships. Establishing appropriate boundaries is essential not only for mutual understanding but also for fostering growth with those we call friends. When we neglect to set these boundaries, we risk outgrowing each other, leading to distance, withdrawal, and isolation. Unconsciously, we detach ourselves from unwanted emotions, situations, and circumstances, gradually embracing inner peace and tranquility.

In my view, boundaries precede expectations. It is imperative to lay down boundaries first, followed by clear expectations. For instance, if my goal is to invest in blue-chip stocks for financial stability, I will refrain from participating in social gatherings that may distract me from achieving my objectives. By stating, "Please don't ask me to join your functions so I can remain focused," I establish a verbal boundary, leaving no room for misunderstanding.

When evaluating friendships, it is crucial to consider whether individuals contribute to our growth. Reflecting on our goals and theirs allows us to assess compatibility and mutual support. Most successful friendships are rooted in a shared purpose, encompassing affection, security, stability, and knowledge.

Since 2015, engaging in conversations with insightful individuals has enriched my mindset and influenced my behavior. By observing their conduct, I gleaned invaluable lessons and identified mentors who became pivotal figures in my life. Their energy and guidance have fostered loyal, trustworthy friendships, illustrating the reciprocity inherent in leadership. Great leaders impart qualities that empower others to expand and grow, perpetuating a legacy or even catalyzing change on a global scale.

Identifying potential friends may be straightforward, but the true test lies in applying this understanding. Embracing this challenge with determination allows us to cultivate meaningful connections that contribute to our personal growth and collective well-being.

CHAPTER IV

Weaknesses

Improvement is impossible
without change.
—John C. Maxwell

What are your weaknesses? Do you have healthy sleep patterns? Do you embrace healthy eating habits? Do you strive to educate yourself regularly, gaining "useful" knowledge? Are there any unhealthy habits that you often indulge in such as excessive drinking, smoking, or abusing drugs? When you commit to these behaviors, or the lack of others, it makes it extremely difficult to unleash your full potential.

The time you spend neglecting yourself is the time you take away from being able to excel in life. You tend to commit to people, places, and situations that are a mere distraction, causing you to entertain fools, foolishness, and foolery. As we grow we must maintain vigilance when adversity comes forth in our life. The first step to improving oneself is to reflect on why you want better.

Exposing and accepting your weaknesses will help you grow and ultimately persevere. Change isn't easy, but it is necessary in our lives. As humans we must strive to advance and march forward toward greatness no matter what obstacles are in our way.

There are many things that will catch my eye, but there are only a few things that will catch my heart.
—Tim Redmond

CHAPTER V

Family

No man can climb out beyond the limitations of his own character.
—John Morley

The bond created among generations is beauty in its purest form. The love, affection, and joy that arise when certain people are connected is priceless. Family isn't restricted to relatives but relatively dissected as a person or group of people who have the same values. Constricted around loyalty, respect, integrity, and honor.

As we experience life, there are situations that allow us to embrace people based on the significance of what they have gone through *together*. Some of these experiences can be in the form of sharing thoughts through conversations or through long-term relationships revolved around consistency and reliability.

There are many other experiences, and by acknowledging these different scenarios, it can give a brief understanding of how to label people as family. Taking the time to understand people whom you love is imperative. The longer you grow together, the stronger the bond will be and the longer the journey together.

When children are young, as adults we must implement and exercise patience as well as discipline within ourselves. Presenting a model behavior is appropriate because of the influence that we have on them. To instill prestige behavior in children, we must exhibit prestige behavior ourselves. Implementing healthy habits and helping our children expose their talents, as well as their purpose in life, is the ideal approach in aiding our youth.

Who you are dictates what you see.
—John C. Maxwell

CHAPTER VI

Hobbies

With enough momentum nearly any kind of change is possible.
—John C. Maxwell

When was the last time you enjoyed something that you love to do? Or better yet when did you last make time enjoy the things you love doing? For some it may be reading, skating, playing sports, traveling, gardening, or baking. Having hobbies is essential to your growth. It helps you find peace, and it can also help eliminate distractions. As we gradually begin to understand what is needed for us to capitalize on growth, we open our imaginations to ponder what truly makes us happy.

When indulging in the things that create happiness, it trickles down to behaviors that not only soothe us but also create harmony within the world around us. Embrace something you love to do! Encourage yourself to make the time to experience the things you love or the things you feel you're missing in your life. This approach can create a sense of relief and satisfaction in your life. You will no longer live in chaotic or frantic environments that take away your peace and tranquility.

CHAPTER VII

Strengths

*A leader is one who sees more than others see, who sees
farther than others see, and who sees before others do.*
—Leroy Eims

Understanding what your strengths are will allow you to appreciate what your purpose is in life. One of my agendas in my life is to give back not only to the people I love but also to humanity. It is important for me to share beliefs, feelings, and ideas with the world so that I can grow with everyone who also wants to experience greatness within themselves.

Identifying your strengths is also essential because as we focus on what we are great at, we can unite and accomplish things we never imagined! For instance, you may be a great listener who can help others find solutions to their problems. Or maybe you're an excellent speaker who has the ability to deliver a message to people and create the influence that can change the world. You could also be an individual who is able to visualize situations before they even occur, saving time by redirecting the focus to resolve other things.

In essence, all these are examples of leaders who implement what they are good at to create a name and build a legacy. Find your strengths, and learn how to master them to improve your life and the world around you!

The secret of success in life is for a man to be ready for his opportunity when it comes.

—Benjamin Disraeli

CONCLUSION

*Humans who strive for victory have no Plan B. That,
in essence, keeps them fighting for greatness.*
—Brandon Brooks

The Warrior Challenge
*It is suggested that you flush your digestive
system before entering this challenge.*

NO SOCIAL MEDIA	EAT LEAN PROTEINS
NO TELEVISION	EAT WHOLE GRAIN
NO SODA	EAT VEGETABLES
NO SUGAR	EAT NUTS
NO ARTIFICIAL SUGARS	EAT FRUITS
NO SALT	DRINK WATER (90 PERCENT INTAKE)
NO SALT SEASONINGS	DRINK FAT-FREE MILK
NO BEEF	

WRITE DOWN YOUR GOALS
MAKE TIME TO REFLECT
SLEEP SEVEN TO TEN HOURS DAILY

ABOUT THE AUTHOR

Brandon, a visionary born in 1990, hails from Baltimore, Maryland. His journey has forged him into a determined entrepreneur, specializing in investments within the stock market. He fearlessly tackles challenges, constantly seeking personal growth through learning and engaging with diverse perspectives. Brandon Brooks stands as a symbol of unwavering dedication to his craft. His commitment to self-improvement is evident through his application of the 14 Laws of Growth, focusing on enhancing thoughts and behaviors. Reading and connecting with knowledgeable individuals from various walks of life contribute to his wealth of insights. In essence, Brandon's mission is to inspire a global community to unlock and pursue their life's passions. His stoic demeanor and commitment to meaningful growth serve as a testament to the indomitable spirit that defines him.

CONTACT INFORMATION

Instagram:
@WALNUTBOTTOMINVESTMENTS

Email:
WALNUTBOTTOMINVESTMENTS@GMAIL.COM

Milton Keynes UK
Ingram Content Group UK Ltd.
UKHW050252280324
440097UK00006B/33